A SUGARLOAF READER

A Cultural History of Sugar

Lawrence Maniscalco

Sugarloaf Ridge State Park History Docent

CONTENTS

FOREWORD	3
ACKNOWLEDGEMENTS	4
A BIRD'S-EYE VIEW OF SUGARLOAF	5
HISTORICAL MILESTONES	6
OUR FIRST INHABITANTS - THE WAPPO	11
HOMESTEADS & HOMESTEADERS	16
THE CHARRING OF SUGARLOAF	24
THE GENTLEMEN RANCHERS	30
WHERE IS LAKE SUGARLOAF?	32
SUGARLOAF BECOMES A PARK	35
HUNTERS, HIPPIES, HIKERS & HAUNTS	42
SUGARLOAF IN ITS GOLDEN YEARS	52
REFERENCES	54

FOREWORD

Sugar wasn't always sold in the neat packages that we buy at our local grocery outlet. Before the turn of the 20th century, sugar came in loaves that looked something like oversize, upside-down ice cream cones. The merchant simply broke off the pieces needed by the customers who, when at home, usually employed scissor-like implements called sugar nips to snip off and granulate the amounts of sweetener they needed. Due to the ubiquity of the cone-shaped product, more than 500 landforms world-wide, including our park, were named after the so-called sugarloaf. (A photograph of the cone-shaped ridge that gave Sugarloaf Ridge State Park its name is pictured on the cover of this book.)

There is another kind of sweetness about this park, and that is its rich cultural history - a history that includes habitation by at least one Native American tribe, scores of hardscrabble homesteaders, often-absent gentleman ranchers, and an occasional sprinkling of hunters, hippies, charcoal-producing colliers, Boy Scouts and Campfire Girls. Their stories unfold in the following pages of this narrative.

The foundation for this book includes the previous historical work of California State Department of Parks and Recreation employees, as well as my own research as a park volunteer. I have attempted to knit these disparate patches of history together into a whole cloth, which I hope will give the reader a better appreciation of the public treasure that we know as Sugarloaf Ridge State Park.

L.M.

ACKNOWLEDGEMENTS

Several people helped to make this cultural history of Sugarloaf Ridge State Park possible. John Roney, who manages the park for Team Sugarloaf, started the process by accepting me as a volunteer to assist with the task of researching and organizing the history of the park. Edward "Breck" Parkman, a former senior archeologist with the Department of Parks and Recreation, was of immense help in identifying areas for research and existing resources, including his own professional studies and insights. Inga Aksamit, a park volunteer and published author, patiently guided me in the use of the park's electronic archive and the mechanics of book publication.

I am grateful for the generosity of a number of people who agreed to be interviewed or to otherwise share their knowledge and resources on a variety of subjects covered in this historical review. They include park volunteers Jeff Falconer, Dave Chalk, Jim Ouimette and Bill Myers; and Sonoma County residents Patrick McMurtry, Diane Besida, Doug Dempster, Jay Gamel, John Frediani, and former Ranger Robyn Ishimatsu. Thanks, as well, to Bay Area District Superintendent Vince Anibale and to Museum Curator Carol Dodge for entrusting me with the entire collection of the park Rangers' daily diaries.

Finally, I would like to thank Sue Cooper, Nancy Evers Kirwin and Tom Murray for volunteering to serve as manuscript editors and for proving to me that one cannot accurately proofread one's own work.

A BIRDS-EYE VIEW OF SUGALOAF

Sugarloaf Ridge State Park is located northeast of Kenwood in the Mayacamas Mountains between the Sonoma and Napa valleys. The original park boundaries comprising 1,560 acres have expanded to a present size of 5,100 acres through a series of land acquisitions. Elevations range from 600 feet at the park entrance to 2,729 feet at the top of Bald Mountain. From there, on a clear day, one can observe panoramic views of the Sierra Nevada and San Francisco Bay.

Hikers along the park's 25 miles of trails pass through two distinct ecological systems - one featuring chaparral-covered ridges and the other marked by linear groves of trees and large open meadows along the Sonoma Creek drainage. Trees in the park include big-leaf maples, coast madrones, California laurels, digger pines, Douglas-firs, alders, California buckeyes, coast redwoods, and several varieties of live and deciduous oaks. Chaparral plants are manzanita, chamise, California lilac, coyote bush, toyon and winebush, along with poison oak and stinging nettles. Sonoma Creek begins in the park and runs for three miles through its southern portion before continuing on to its southeastern terminus in San Pablo Bay.

The poet Ralph Waldo Emerson once wrote that "the earth laughs in flowers." In the spring, Sugarloaf Ridge State Park comes alive with wildflowers - California poppies, cream cups, lupine, penstemon, buttercups, and varieties of peas, shooting stars, trillium, and Indian warrior. Less common varieties include golden fairy lantern, zigadene and fritillaria. In early summer come clarkia, scarlet larkspur, farewell-to-spring, Mariposa lilies, monkey flowers, and Indian pinks. Yellow star thistles and tarweed are common in late summer.

The park's family campground and picnic area lie in a meadow near Sonoma Creek at 1,200 feet of elevation. The 50 campsites will accommodate trailers and campers up to 22 feet. A group camping area, accommodating up to 100 people, is situated near the Robert Ferguson Observatory, which was established in 1997 as the largest celestial observatory in the western United States completely dedicated to public viewing and education.

HISTORICAL MILESTONES

PREHISTORY

Recent archeological evidence indicates that Sugarloaf Ridge State Park was first inhabited by Native Americans about 7,000 years ago, though studies suggest it could have been much longer.

RECORDED HISTORY

At the time of the Spanish arrival, circa 1770, the area was occupied by Wappo Indians. Their permanent villages were located in the Napa Valley; but during the dry summer months, families would camp in the area of Sugarloaf to take advantage of the food supply provided by deer, smaller game, acorns, seeds and nuts. Their permanent seasonal village was known to the Wappo people as Wilikos.

1800s

The Wappo would not acquiesce to European subjugation; but a cholera epidemic in 1833 followed by a smallpox outbreak in 1838 decimated their numbers.

Scottish sea captain, John (Juan) Wilson, the husband of Ramona Carillo (General Mariano Vallejo's sister-in-law), was awarded in 1837 a Mexican land grant of the 18,833-acre Rancho Guilucos. It was one of 27 such land grants in Sonoma County awarded by the Spanish from 1784 until Mexican independence in 1821, and then by the Mexican government from 1833 until the formation of the California Republic in 1846. The largest land grant in Sonoma County, Rancho Petaluma at 66,622 acres, was awarded to General Vallejo. Wilson's grant was the seventh largest in the county. He never lived on the land, residing instead in grand patriarchal style in the Santa Barbara-San Luis Obispo area where he owned several other ranchos including the 3,167-acre Rancho Canada del Chorro, the Huerta de Romaldo Rancho of 117 acres and the 100,000-acre Rancho Canada de los Osos.

In the early 1840s, Wilson built a single-story 25x18-foot adobe house with 22-inch thick walls on the east bank of Sonoma Creek near the entrance to Adobe Canyon, giving the canyon and the road to the park their names. The cabin was used as a residence, possibly by Wilson's brother-in-law Julio Carrillo, the ranch majordomo. It later was used as a stagecoach stop for the route between Sonoma and Santa Rosa.

In 1850, the rancho was sold to another Scotsman, William Hood, and a partner, William Petit, for $13,000 apiece; in 1854 Hood became sole owner. The name of the rancho was changed to "Los Guilicos" on a land survey in 1859. Hood probably lived for a time in the old adobe house built by Wilson, until the foundation for his 29-room Hood House was laid in 1858.

The few remaining Wappo were either killed by white settlers or placed on the Mendocino Reservation by 1856, thus marking the end of the already-diminished Wilikos.

The area now occupied by Sugarloaf Ridge State Park remained uninhabited until homesteading began in 1866, under the Homestead Act of 1862. On May 1, 1867, John D. Bowen patented the first homestead in the area of the park. His 160-acre homestead was just outside the present south boundary of the park above the campground. It now is covered by a vineyard belonging to the Thacher family. According to the park's first Ranger, Milo Shepard, many of the Scots, Irish and German homesteaders who farmed and ranched on the hillsides around the park were here because the rich valley lands were in Mexican land grants and the remaining lowlands were too swampy to cultivate.

Sonoma Valley was served by two railroad lines: the narrow-gauge Sonoma Valley branch of the San Francisco & North Pacific Railroad Company and the standard-gauge Santa Rosa and Carquinez Railroad, a subsidiary of Southern Pacific. The railroads initially provided for the transport of the area's desirable basalt paving stones, and later carried agricultural products and passengers bound for the valley's wineries and spas.

The Luttrell family might have been among the first owners of the property that is now Sugarloaf Ridge State Park. By 1880, the older generation of the family, Congressman John King and Samantha Luttrell, consolidated the homesteads in the main valley of Sugarloaf Ridge for the purpose of producing charcoal from the oak and madrone hardwood forests that covered the valley floor and hillsides. After harvesting the hardwood forests between 1887 and 1893, the Luttrell's 640-acre holdings reverted to the San Francisco Savings and Loan Society. Charcoal production continued on the subsequently-owned Reynolds Ranch, possibly until the early 20th century.

1900s

On April 10, 1907, W.D. Reynolds purchased a 640-acre tract from John W. and Hettie Jane Warboys, and constructed a ranch complex including a two-bedroom house, two barns and several other buildings (one barn and a garage, used as a shop, still remain at the park operation area). He also developed the main spring that supplies all of the water for the park today. Reynolds expanded the ranch to 1,040 acres and held the property for approximately six years, but his name continued to be linked to the property.

It was on a site near the headwaters of Bear Creek, that Ray and Bertha Hurd homesteaded on 160 acres between 1914 and 1930. The Hurd Ranch started with a 12x12-foot cabin and grew to include a permanent house, a red barn (still standing), a woodshed, and a school house for the education of their children and the children of neighboring families (the Hurds had 11 children between 1903 and 1928, one of whom died at age 11.)

A road was built in 1920 to connect the Hurd ranch to Sonoma Valley. Prior to this event the only access was by foot or horse.

The Sonoma State Home at Eldridge purchased the 1,040-acre Reynolds Ranch on January 5, 1920, with hopes of developing the main valley into a reservoir for a water supply to the Home. However, a 15-year water-rights battle between the downstream residents and the Home blocked development of the reservoir. The completion of Suttonfield Dam on June 21, 1938 near Eldridge solved the chronic water shortage problem at the Home, and ended forever the water rights controversy.

The Hurd Ranch was sold in 1930 and subsequently used as a deer hunting club (the remains of the club's butchering shed still can be seen near the red barn). The property later was leased out and was for a time in the 1960s inhabited on a semi-regular basis by hippie groups, perhaps unknown to the landlord.

In 1931, the Sonoma State Home established Camp Butler. Named for Dr. Frederick Otis Butler, the State Home's Superintendent from 1918 to 1949, it was a combined Boy Scout and Campfire Girls camp for the residents of the Home. It consisted of a cookhouse with a large patio made of wood rounds, a tractor-dug, slate-lined swimming pool with a diving board, and a parade ground with a flag pole, all located below the Reynolds spring overlooking the Reynolds Ranch complex where the caretaker lived.

The shortage of fuel and staff caused by the outbreak of World War II forced the closure of Camp Butler on November 9, 1942. After the end of WW II, the patients of the Home were limited to the more severely developmentally disabled and handicapped, and the scouting program never was re-started.

The Reynolds Ranch was leased for cattle grazing and hunting to Wesley (Dutch) and Vivian (Toad) Pfister on July 1, 1943. The subsequent lessees of the property were John Elgard (1948-51), Frank and Virginia Monnich (1951-53), and the Raffo Brothers Milk Transport Company of Glen Ellen (1953-64).

In 1959, the Reynolds Ranch was declared surplus property. Its immediate public sale was prevented by the review of state lands for the placement of a North Bay Area state college. This allowed time for public and political forces to martial efforts to make the property a state park.

On September 24, 1964, the Reynolds Ranch, now expanded to 1,520 aces, was transferred to the California Division of Beaches and Parks and designated as "Sugarloaf Ridge State Park."

In December of that year, Long Beach oilman Clinton A. Petrie, on his way to a rendezvous with potential investors in Santa Rosa in a winter storm with zero visibility, crashed his Cessna 310 into the top of a ridge near Brushy Peaks in the park.

In 1968, the Hurd Ranch home burned to the ground, apparently the result of a candle accident. The house foundation, stairway and chimney remains are visible at the site.

In 1969, after construction of an entry road, a campground, and the destruction of most of the Reynolds Ranch buildings, Sugarloaf Ridge State Park was opened to the public on Memorial Day weekend under the direction of resident Ranger, Milo Shepard, the great-grandnephew of Jack London.

On July 7, 1970, Pacific Telephone and Telegraph transferred 49.7 acres around Red Mountain to Sugarloaf Ridge State Park for an access route to the top, and constructed a telephone microwave station on their remaining five-acre parcel at the summit.

In 1971, the State of California purchased the Hurd Ranch red barn. In the same year, the entire Bear Creek Ranch and the 80-acre Malm Flat Ranch were added to the park, and telephone service finally reached Sugarloaf.

In 1972, 40 acres just west of the campground owned by Barbara K. Von Tillow were added to Sugarloaf Ridge State Park.

In 1973, 150 acres owned by Robert W. Ragle along the west boundary of the park were acquired. That property added ¼ mile of Adobe Canyon Road to the park, and included the summit of Sugarloaf Ridge.

In 1979, a program was initiated by Margery Stern with The Trust for Public Lands to transfer approximately 330 acres of her ranch west of Bear Creek in small parcels to Sugarloaf Ridge State Park, to be completed by 1988. Along with sixty-plus acres purchased from a Mr. Fiorentino, a complete connection was made between Sugarloaf Ridge State Park and Hood Mountain Regional Park.

At 1:25 p.m. on January 31, 1984, electricity finally arrived at Sugarloaf Ridge State Park.

In 1985, 40 acres of the Bureau of Land Management land in Napa County along the eastern boundary of Sugarloaf Ridge State Park and 52.2 acres known as the Harr Ranch, next to Hood Mountain Regional Park west of Bear Creek, were added to the park. The Harr family retained tenancy rights until 1988.

In 1987, the Visitor Center was constructed near the campground entrance.

During the two-day observance of the worldwide "Harmonic Convergence" on August 16-17, 1987, Sugarloaf Ridge State Park enjoyed the locally-determined status of a "power center." More than 1,000 persons assembled in the park on August 16 to join in an event that sought to involve 144,000 persons around the world all meditating for peace.

During the 1990s, 1,100 acres of the McCormick Ranch were incorporated into the park, bringing the total park acreage to approximately 4,000 acres.

In 1997, the Robert Ferguson Observatory was constructed in the group camp area. The RFO is the largest celestial observatory in the western United States completely dedicated to public viewing and education.

2000s

In response to the threatened closure of 55 California state parks due to budgetary considerations, including Sugarloaf Ridge State Park, a group of five conservation groups in 2012 entered into an operating agreement with the State of California to operate Sugarloaf for a seven-year period. Known as Team Sugarloaf, the five groups included the Sonoma County Ecology Center, the Valley of the Moon Observatory Association, United Camps, Conferences and Retreats, the Valley of the Moon Natural History Association, and the Sonoma County Trails Council.

In October 2017, the worst series of fires in California history to that date engulfed a large section of Sonoma County, including three-quarters of Sugarloaf Ridge State Park, forcing its closure until February 1, 2018. There was extensive damage to park assets including the destruction of four houses, two barns and two sheds at the Stern Ranch, one house at the Harr Ranch, two bathrooms in the main camp ground, three bridges, 50 steps on Canyon and Vista trails, 12 retaining walls, and a water tank on Hillside Trail.

OUR FIRST INHABITANTS - THE WAPPO

The name Wappo is believed to be based upon the Spanish word *guapo*, which can mean harsh, severe, daring, or brave. Tradition has it that the Wappo - normally a gentle people - were harsh, severe, daring, and brave in opposing the Spanish invasion of their lands and the destruction of their culture. This etymology seems slightly questionable, but no better one has been offered. In any case, the name probably was not used by the Indians themselves. They are said to have called themselves, at least within their village habitats, "the people who speak plainly and truthfully, the outspoken ones."

According to Breck Parkman, former Senior State Archeologist and Tribal Liaison with the California Department of Parks and Recreation, the Wappo had their permanent villages in the Napa Valley. The Sugarloaf area represented a hinterland claimed by the Wappo, but not always inhabited by them. During wet winter months the area was all but abandoned, but with the advent of summer, Sugarloaf's forests of oak and herds of deer provided a good food supply of acorns, seeds, nuts, venison, and small game. The oldest known archaeological evidence of Wappo habitation at Sugarloaf dates to more than 7,000 years ago. Much older sites probably exist, but have yet to be discovered. Five major habitation sites have been found in the valley near Sugarloaf Ridge State Park, which together represents a major permanent seasonal village known as Wilicos.

The Wappo had a very simple culture - one of the simplest in North America. They were without writing, metals, agriculture, pottery, or domestic animals. Their life has been described as colorless simplicity. Linguistically, the Wappo affiliate with the Yuki, Coast Yuki and Huchnom; but their dialect differed as much from that of the Yuki as does German from English.

Their sociopolitical unit was the village, which was usually located on a creek or near other sources of water. A typical Wappo village consisted of up to 40 oval-shaped huts constructed of poles and thatch. Some were as large as 30 feet long, where each family had its own door, smoke hole, and fire pit. (See illustrations at right and below.) Dried ferns and grasses were used as pillows, and roof poles held baskets and food supplies. Every settlement had a dance house, and a dome-shaped sweathouse located near a stream. Men used the sweathouse once or twice daily, and then plunged into the nearby cold waters. Women could not use the sweathouse, but bathed each morning in the cold waters of a creek or nearby stream.

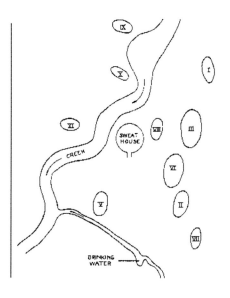

A typical Wappo grass hut

In appearance, both men and women wore their hair long. While men went almost naked, women wore double aprons of softened deerskin. In the winter, both men and women were protected from the elements by rabbit-skin or bear-skin capes. No shoes or hats were worn.

The Wappo were said to be kind and self-effacing. Children were "spoiled," and could be raised by any senior female relative who was no longer fertile. They held firmly to land and family, but property was essentially a disfavored concept.

All family members worked at gathering food, net-weaving, and making clothing and finely-wrought coiled willow baskets. Basketry was one of the arts of life in which the Wappo excelled. Their work was in every way comparable to that of the neighboring Pomo, who have been judged as the finest basket makers in the world. (See a Wappo basket at right.) According to Driver, this illustrates the principle that tribes generally low in culture can excel in some special features.

There was very little division of labor among the Wappo. Women and children gathered acorns, roots, tubers and bulbs, while men hunted and fished. An exception was made for "physicians" who served as healers. The Wappo distinguished between the doctor or shaman who obtained his power from supernatural experience (the so-called Sucking or Dreaming doctor), and the one whose methods were essentially magical (the Singing or Outfit doctor).

The Wappo depended more on vegetable than on animal foods. The acorn was their most important single food source. The deer was the chief animal game, although small game such as rabbits, squirrels, rats, birds, and grasshoppers probably provided more food year-round than did the deer.

Marriage was monogamous. There was no bride purchase, and the marriage ceremony consisted of an equal exchange of gifts between the merging families. Marriage was prohibited between all known blood relatives. Divorce was by mutual consent, but was uncommon. Women gave birth in a menstrual room, with a female relative assisting as midwife. The Wappo practiced a phenomenon known as "couvade" in which the father, at the birth of a child, would lie down in the main part of the house for four days and could not smoke, talk loud, or eat meat, fish or fat. On the fifth and succeeding days, he could resume his normal activities. The dead were cremated. Sometimes a bereaved wife would attempt to throw herself on the funeral pyre, but she always was restrained by a relative. A widow might marry her deceased husband's brother, or a widower his deceased wife's sister.

A chief was nominally "in charge" and could be elected, appointed, or chosen to fill a needed function. Depending upon the need and the particular interests of the tribe, there could be more than one chief at one time. Four functions generally were served by the chiefs: internal functioning of the village; relations with other villages, including warfare; dances, ceremonies and medicine; and the transmission of news and information. When a woman was chief - and there were several - her function was somewhat curtailed, in that she would not have ordinarily directed male activities. The position of chief was held until death.

Warfare was rare among these gentle folk and, when it occurred, was usually the result of a serious protest, a threat to one's life, or to avenge a wrongdoing. Skirmishes with the Spanish, however, involved larger numbers with as many as 10 deaths. Even so, these "full-scale" battles ended when an important person was killed or when the sun went down.

The Wappo believed in a Great Spirit or Supreme Being. Four was a sacred number and was used in rituals with prayers to bring harmony between the universe and the people. The Wappo had names for stars and constellations. The tribe had a special storyteller, who told the people around the fire pit the tales and legends of the heavenly stars. The year was divided into four seasons and twelve moons. The moons were recorded with sticks, which were also used in counting. Besides the four cardinal directions, up and down were recognized. This was the limit of their abstract knowledge.

<u>Wappo Celestial Phenomena</u>

Sun: hin-tume (day sun -male)
Moon: utcuwamehin (night sun - male)
Morning star: keu-soke (female)
Evening star: sum-soke (female)
Big dipper: tc'ena (long pole with hook)
Little dipper: so'tsema
Milky Way: hote'umits (ghost road)
Eclipse: hini-tcae'mse (sun lost)

Full moon: hin-mopila (moon full)
New moon: hin-ciits (moon new)
Rainbow: cini-la'-kama (colors spread)
Whirlwind: oma-metili (caused by ghosts; made person's body swell up if it struck him)

Wappo Time Periods

Year: oma-wen (world season)

Wappo Seasons

Spring: oma'tc'utsasi
Summer: helu-wen (fire season)
Fall: oma-te-tsawo-inca (world grass top?)
Winter: tsa'-wena (end season)

Wappo Months

January: pipo-tso-hin (white oak earth moon)
February: kotico-pele-hin (black oak leaves moon)
March: pipo-pele-hin (white oak leaves moon)
April: hin-yawela (moon no-name)
May: wa'ate-hin (pinole moon)
June: t'oltcuk-hin (burn-the-valley moon)
July: tcano-hin (manzanita moon)
August: mel-hin-yawela (acorn moon no-name)
September: mel-hin (acorn moon)
October: mel-cimatisai-hin (acorn leaves cover moon)
November: hol-pele-hin (wood leaves moon)
December: holma-pele-hin (brush leaves moon)

Wappo Periods of the Day

Morning: kewutci
Noon: hinta howa'e (sun divide)
Afternoon or evening: sumu
Sunset: su'muwa
Getting dark: tcitcise
Night: hutcuwa
Midnight: hutcu howa'e (night divide)

Wappo Directions

North: muti
South: wen
East: helup
West: wita
Up: met
Down: tso (Earth)

Twelve sticks were used to keep track of the months. The chief threw one away at each last quarter when the moon was almost gone. Sticks also were given to another village with a feast invitation - as many sticks as there were days before feast. The prospective guests threw away one stick each day. Any brief time period was recorded in this way. Sticks also were used to keep score in games and for ordinary counting. The Wappo employed sticks of only one size, and were not accustomed to large numbers. The Pomo, on the other hand, used sticks of three sizes and were said to have counted as high as 40,000.

The Wappo were eventually decimated by a cholera epidemic in 1833, followed by a smallpox outbreak five years later. Prior to that time, the Wappo had numbered about 8,000 people; but by 1850 there were fewer than 500. Several of those survivors were forced onto a reservation in the Mendocino area, near Covelo.

Today, the descendants of the Mishewal Wappo band from Alexander Valley are trying to reclaim tribal recognition, which had been terminated by the federal government in 1959.

HOMESTEADS & HOMESTEADERS

The first non-indigenous American people came to the Valley of the Moon in 1810. At that time, California was in the hands of the Spanish, who established their last mission in Sonoma in 1823, two years after Mexico won its independence from Spain. Soon the Mexicans were the predominant force. In 1833, General Mariano Vallejo was sent to establish a pueblo (town) near Mission San Francisco de Solano and marched his small band of soldiers around the countryside, in part to warn American settlers and the Russians at Fort Ross of Mexico's ownership and resolve.

The Mexicans, like the Spanish before them, encouraged settlement of California by giving prominent persons land grants called *ranchos*, which were to be used for grazing or cultivated as farms. There were 27 such land grants given in Sonoma County. The largest of these, the 66,622-acre Petaluma Adobe, was awarded to General Vallejo. The 7th largest grant - the 18,333-acre Rancho Guilucos - was given to John Wilson, a Scots sea captain who courted and married Vallejo's sister-in-law, Ramona Carillo, and changed his name to Juan to obtain Mexican citizenship and eventual grants of land. Wilson never lived on his Sonoma rancho, which encompassed what now is Hood Mountain Regional Park, the village of Oakmont, and Trione-Annadel State Park. He resided instead in grand patriarchal fashion in central California, where he owned several other ranchos.

In 1850, Rancho Guilucos was sold to another Scotsman, William Hood, and a partner William Pettit. In 1854, Hood became the sole owner, eventually changing the name of the rancho to Los Guilicos. The war with Mexico in 1846 and eventual statehood in 1850 ended Mexican hegemony. According to treaty, the Mexican land grants were honored if title could be confirmed. In time, rancheros became land rich and cash poor. Unable to defend their claims or pay mortgages, many ranchos were sold to Americans, and were quickly subdivided and sold to new settlers.

None of the land within the present boundaries of Sugarloaf Ridge State Park was included in the Mexican land grant award system, due in part to the difficulty of cultivation in the high Mayacamas Ridge. However, the cultural history of the park does include an agrarian component, which began with the lure of free government land for the establishment of small farms called homesteads.

THE HOMESTEAD ACT

On the first day of 1863, President Abraham Lincoln signed into law the Homestead Act of 1862. That landmark piece of legislation would provide the stimulus for the establishment of an estimated two million small farms on 270,000,000 acres - about 10 percent of all land in the United States - speeding settlement of the nation and privatizing ownership of much of the country.

The passage of the 1862 Homestead Act allowed settlement of public lands, and required only proof of residence with improvement and cultivation of the land. Any citizen or person intending to become a citizen, who was at least 21 years of age and the head of a household, and who had not taken up arms against the United States government or given aid or comfort to its enemies, could make application. (See a sample application below.)

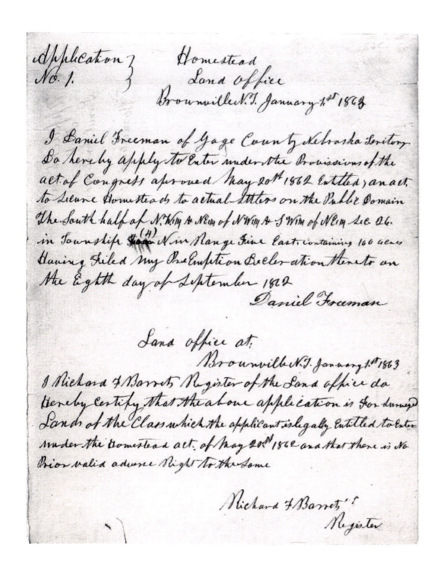

This latter provision excluded all of the citizens of the Confederacy from participation; but their rights under the act were restored at the end of the Civil War and in the 1866 revision of the Homestead Act. With five years residence, and improvements and cultivation of the land, an applicant could receive up to 160 acres free and clear with only a $15 fee.

PROOF REQUIRED UNDER HOMESTEAD ACTS MAY 20, 1862, AND JUNE 21, 1866.

WE, Joseph Graff & Samuel Kilpatrick do solemnly swear that we have known Daniel Inman for over five years last past; that he is the head of a family consisting of wife and two children and is — a citizen of the United States; that he is an inhabitant of the S½ of NW¼ & NE of NW¼ & SW¼ of NE¼ of section No. 26 in Township No. 4 N of Range No. 5 E and that no other person resided upon the said land entitled to the right of Homestead or Pre-emption.

That the said Daniel Inman — entered upon and made settlement on said land on the 1st day of January, 1863, and has built a house thereon part log & part frame 14 by 20 feet one story, with two doors two windows, shingle roof board floor and is a comfortable house to live in

and has lived in the said house and made it his exclusive home from the 1st day of January, 1863, to the present time, and that he has since said settlement ploughed, fenced, and cultivated about 35 — acres of said land, and has made the following improvements thereon, to wit: built a Stable, a Sheep shed 100 feet long Corn crib, and has 40 apple and about 400 peach trees set out.

Joseph Graff
Samuel Kilpatrick

I, Henry M. Atkinson Register do hereby certify that the above affidavit was taken and subscribed before me this 20th day of January, 1868.

Henry M. Atkinson
Register

WE CERTIFY that Joseph Graff & Samuel Kilpatrick whose names are subscribed to the foregoing affidavit, are persons of respectability.

Henry M. Atkinson, Register.
Jno L. Carson, Receiver.

HOMESTEADING IN SUGARLOAF

There were 4,046 homestead declarations filed in Sonoma County between the years 1860 and 1921. Government Land Office archives in the online resources of the Bureau of Land Management identified no fewer than 68 homesteads in and around the area that is now Sugarloaf Ridge State Park. The map below shows the approximate location of those homesteads. The present boundaries of the park are shown within the lined area.

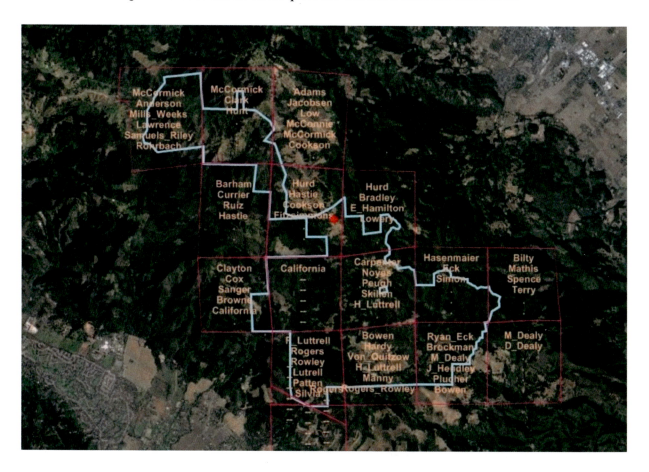

John D. Bowen is reputed to have been the first homesteader in the area of the park. His 160-acre homestead, which was patented on May 1, 1867, was located just outside the south boundary of the park above the campground. It now is covered by a vineyard owned by the Thacher family. The U.S. Census for 1880 includes an entry for a John D. Bowen, who is listed as a white 54-year old single male from Pennsylvania, who was employed as a farmer. As well, in the Glen Ellen section of the 1903 Santa Rosa City Directory, the name of a John D. Bowen is listed as a farmer. If these sources are accurate, Bowen would have been 41 years old when he received the land patent for his homestead.

Other homesteads of historic interest in the vicinity of the park include the Luttrell, McCormick, Fitzsimmons, Hamilton, and Cookson homesteads, whose properties have expanded the original boundaries of the park. The homestead that is of greatest significance to the cultural history of the park is, no doubt, the Hurd family homestead also known as the Bear Creek Ranch. The site of the Hurds' homestead today is accessible to hikers in the park who walk the various routes to Bald Mountain, and then descend the High Ridge Trail for approximately one mile to the remains of the Hurd family's permanent home and the intact and picturesque red barn.

THE HURD HOMESTEAD

In 1914, Ray and Bertha Hurd loaded their household goods and the first six of their 10 surviving children onto a horse-drawn wagon, and began the short but arduous journey from Napa Valley  to their permanent home on a rugged 160-acre parcel of land on the far side of the Mayacamas Ridge near Bear Creek. When the dirt road ran out, they continued up the mountain by foot, packing their belongings on their backs or on sleds behind the horses. Their first task was to construct a home. It was only a 12x12-foot wood shake cabin with a dirt floor (see photo left). It would be followed later by a larger and more permanent house and a large red barn (see photo below), as well as improvements to the land which would meet the provisions of the Homestead Act. By 1920, the Hurds would have secured their right to ownership of the property.

The Hurds were typical of many of the Midwestern homesteaders in Sonoma County. Ray Hurd was born in Iowa on September 28, 1878 and died at age 96 on September 4, 1975 in Napa. He was one of seven children. His father, Thomas D. Hurd (1838-1927), was born in Olean, N.Y.;

his mother, Anna Agustus Wilhemina Menge (1850-1929), was born in Germany and died in Sebastopol.

Bertha Alice Hurd (nee Saunders) was born in Bridgewater, South Dakota on June 28, 1883, and died near Blue Lake, California on July 12, 1956. Her father and mother were born in South Dakota. Bertha had six sisters, one of whom, Myrtle Cookson, lived on the nearby Cookson homestead, north of the Hurd ranch on the Napa side of the Mayacamas Ridge. A second sister, with the surname Harrison, lived on the Vertosa ranch on the north side of Bald Mountain by Silver Oaks.

Bertha married Ray Hurd in 1901 and gave birth to eleven children, one of whom (Clarence) died at birth. The Hurd progeny included Raymond, the eldest, born in 1902, and his siblings Ralph (1904), Fern Hurd Williams (1905), Hazel Hurd Harding (1907), Edwin (also called Jim, 1909), Grace Hurd Williams (1911), Pearl Hurd Mora (1914), Francis (1921), Irma Hurd Mitchell (1925), and Alvin (1927). Ray and Bertha had 24 grandchildren and 25 great-grandchildren. The size of the extended Hurd clan was estimated in 1981 to be 682 persons; and family reunions held at the Bear Creek ranch attracted as many as 200 people.

Former Senior State Archeologist Breck Parkman has described life at the Bear Creek Ranch from its beginning in 1914 to when it was sold in 1930: "The family was almost completely self-sufficient, due in part to their geographic isolation. They raised a few cows and had chickens and turkeys, and they grew vegetables in a small garden (turnip, beet, radish, corn, etc.). A small orchard, including walnuts and apricots, was planted near the house and a fruit cellar was dug nearby. The family did a lot of canning and they put away dried apples and sweet corn. Bertha cooked on a big wood range, which also heated the house. During deer hunting season, when hunters roamed the local hills, she would often cook for the hunters, feeding them at the family's dining table.

"Because the children had to be away all week, attending school down in the Napa Valley, Ray in 1916 constructed a small schoolhouse at the homestead, and then hired a teacher who lived with the family as if she were a part of it. From then on, the kids went to their own school until they were in high school. [Note: There were approximately 35 people living on neighboring ranches, including two children on the Cookson ranch (the Hurd children's cousins Samuel and Leonard) and two children on the Fitzsimmons ranch.]

"When accidents occurred, and there were definitely a few of those, Bertha took care of the injuries. One of her children, Alvin, almost cut off his foot on a broken bottle; and another, Francis, almost bit his tongue in two. A third child, Grace, was bitten by a rattlesnake. In all of these cases, Bertha took immediate action. For Alvin's cut foot, she stopped the bleeding by pouring sugar into the wound, allowing her the necessary time to get him to the doctor. She treated little Grace's snakebite all by herself, with no trip necessary to see the doctor.

"In 1917, another of Ray and Bertha's children, Raymond Jr. (photo at left at age 19), lost his leg in an accident at the naval shipyard on Mare Island. He came back to the homestead and secluded himself there for the next three years, self-conscious of his missing limb. A few years later, a neighbor decided to end his life. He placed a lit stick of dynamite on a stump, and then sat down beside it to keep it company. Afterwards, the son of the dead man came to live with the family. [Note: The neighbor's name was thought to have been Johnson, possibly a ranch hand on the Fitzsimmons ranch.]

"In the early 1920s, the family with the help of a neighbor constructed a road that would allow them access to the Sonoma Valley. In the 1920s, though, this area was being used as a nudist retreat, one of the earliest such camps in northern California. The road passed near this unseen camp, and it was the cause of great speculation among the kids, as evidenced in an interview conducted with three of them in 1983.

"In 1930, Ray and Bertha sold their property to a businessman who lived in the Napa Valley. The new owner used the property as a deer hunting club and added a new structure or two of his own, including a deer dressing shed complete with a 1942 date and the print of a deer hoof scratched into the concrete floor. In time, the property changed hands once again* and was later leased out to several different tenants. In 1967, more than 30 'hippies' are said to have been living on the ranch; and it was estimated by a neighbor that as many as 90 people spent the weekends there. During a weekend in 1968, the old house burned to the ground, apparently the result of an untended candle."

Mr. Parkman in 2016 conducted an archeological investigation of items strewn about the remains of the Bear Creek house and discovered some items of clothing that, in this author's opinion, were similar to those that were popularized during the hippie era in the 1960s (see photos, next page).

*According to Christina Jones, the property was sold in 1964 to Santa Rosa attorney, Everett Shapiro, who formed Bear Creek Ranch Incorporated as an investment for people who did not use the land. The house was rented or leased, and Shapiro was responsible for opening the road leading to Adobe Canyon Road. Mr. Shapiro thought that the fire that consumed the house in 1968 might have started with a forgotten candle left burning in the bathroom.

 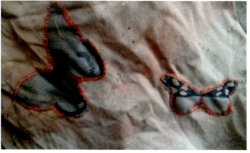

"Hippie" articles of clothing discovered near the ruins of the Hurd house

The State of California purchased the Bear Creek Ranch in two installments in 1971 and 1972.

THE CHARRING OF SUGARLOAF

The mention of the word *charcoal* today conjures up the image of a backyard barbecue fueled by a bank of insignificant lumps of crumbly black material. But to persons a century or so ago, that same word would have triggered thoughts of a high quality and essential commercial product, a vital and job-producing American industry, and even an underlying threat of forest depletion.

During the 19th and early 20th century, wood and coal were the most commonly used sources of energy in California and throughout the United States. California did not have an abundance of naturally occurring coal, and what was available was of such poor quality that much of that kind of fuel had to be imported. Wood was abundant in California's forests and was used to power steam engines, and also used in manufacturing and transportation; but nearly 90% of it was used for domestic heating and cooking. While wood could be used as fuel in its natural state, it could also be converted into charcoal, another source of energy that by 1850 was in demand for blacksmithing and metallurgy. Its light weight, superior heating capacity compared to wood and its ability to burn cleanly without producing sooty smoke, made charcoal an excellent source of fuel for domestic uses, as well.

WHAT IS CHARCOAL?

Charcoal is a material that is obtained by slowly heating wood or other organic substances in the absence of air. It is the absence of air - called *pyrolysis* - that makes the difference by removing moisture and volatile gasses, producing a light, black form of carbon resembling coal. Charcoal burns much hotter (twice the heat of seasoned wood) and more evenly and consistently than wood. In addition to removing water and impurities, carbonization leaves low ash content and a low volume of trace elements like sulfur and phosphorous, meaning that it produces a "clean" heat. As well, charcoal is much easier than wood to transport and store as it has one-third its weight and one-half its volume. The characteristics of good charcoal include hardness, retention of the grain of the wood, a jet-black lustrous color, and a metallic ring when struck. It also is non-soiling, can float in water, and can burn without a flame.

HOW IS CHARCOAL USED?

Charcoal has been used since earliest times for a large range of purposes, but by far its most important use has been as a metallurgical fuel. Charcoal is the traditional fuel of a blacksmith's forge and other applications where an intense heat is required. It is an excellent reducing fuel for the production of iron, and has been used that way since Roman times. Charcoal was the fuel of choice in the early 19th century for iron-making and smelting in the United States. Until the 1830s, all iron in the United States was produced using charcoal as fuel.

In ground-up form, charcoal was important to early chemists and was a constituent of formulas for mixtures such as black powder. Due to its high surface area, charcoal can be used as a filter, a catalyst or an adsorbent. Charcoal is still used in art for drawing and for making rough sketches. In the past, it was consumed as a dietary supplement for gastric problems in the form of charcoal biscuits.

In the late 19th century, San Francisco consumed annually about 3,600 tons of charcoal worth about $65,000 at the rate of $17 a ton. The bulk of the supply came from Sonoma County. The San Francisco Mint alone consumed about 325 tons, and the canneries about 250 tons per year.

HOW IS CHARCOAL MADE?

In Sonoma County, groups of Italian immigrants (called *colliers*) often would contract with landowners to clear their trees in return for the opportunity to make the wood into charcoal, before moving on to the next ranch. Only live trees (e.g. oak, madrone, Douglas-fir) were cut to make charcoal. Leaves, small branches and sometimes the bark were removed in order to maximize the amount of solid wood in the completed pile. The wood was cut into four-foot lengths; and, to keep the pile as uniform as possible, very large pieces were split, so that all the wood was about the same diameter.

Once a sufficient amount had been cut, it was hauled in horse-drawn wagons to a nearby flat that had been leveled from the naturally sloping terrain - often at the "Y" created by the confluence of two small creeks, or on gently sloping alluvial terraces. Deliberately located near water to control the burning process, these flats were 30 to 40 feet in diameter. The soil that had been removed in leveling the flat was kept nearby, and later thrown on top of the pile after the wood had been stacked.

The four-foot long wood was placed in an upright circular fashion around a center pole that later would be removed to create a central chimney, about 12 inches in diameter. The first layer of wood extended about four or five feet from the center; then a second layer, a third layer, and so on, were set until the layered wood formed a circle about 30 to 40 feet in diameter. Next, a second tier and a third tier was stacked, each having a smaller diameter. The completed surface oven, or charcoal oven, resembled a beehive about 10 to 14 feet high.

A charcoal mound under construction, Sonoma County, 1915 (Sonoma County History and Genealogy Library, Photo 29332)

Having completed its construction, the colliers lit the oven by dropping lighted kindling and paper or hot coals and wood chips down the chimney, adding kerosene if needed to encourage the burning. The entire oven was then covered with green Douglas-fir or redwood boughs, followed by six to eight inches of hand-shoveled and packed earth to keep the wood from burning too fast. Small vent holes were located near the base to induce or retard the air needed to draw the burn from the center to the edges of the wood pile.

Then the hard work began.

The key to the production of charcoal was the manipulation of the oven vents, and the collier's ability to determine what was going on inside the oven from external cues. Once lit, the colliers never left the site of the burning until the entire process was finished - a process that often would take four to five weeks to complete. A 30-foot diameter, 14-foot high oven comprised of about

30 cords of wood would have produced approximately 1,000 sacks of charcoal, each weighing 50 to 70 pounds.

A collier tending his charcoal oven, Trenton, CA, 1910 (Sonoma County History and Genealogy Library, Photo 10376)

CHARCOAL-MAKING IN SUGARLOAF

According to Sugarloaf's official historical timeline, two of the earliest residents in the area of the park, J.K. and Samantha Luttrell, had by 1880 consolidated the homesteads in the main valley for the purpose of producing charcoal from the oak and madrone hardwood forests that covered the valley floor and hillsides at that time. The Luttrell's 640-acre holdings eventually reverted to the San Francisco Savings and Loan Society. Charcoal production probably continued during the time that the property was owned and ranched by W.D. Reynolds, who purchased the land in 1907. Emma Bettiga Catelani, who lived for a time on the Reynolds ranch, once told the park's first Ranger Milo Shepard that charcoal was produced on the Reynolds property and hauled off by horse and wagon early in the 20th century.

The full name of J.K. Luttrell was John King Luttrell (1831-1893) who was a Representative from California to the U.S. Congress. He was born near Knoxville, Tennessee and attended the common schools. Luttrell (photo left) moved with his parents to a farm in Alabama in 1844 and to Missouri near St. Joseph in 1845. He moved to California in 1852 and engaged in mining, then settled in Yolo County and engaged in agricultural pursuits. He moved to Prairie City (later Folsom) in 1853, to El Dorado County in 1854, to Watsonville in Santa Cruz County, and then to Alameda County. He studied law, was admitted to the bar, and commenced practice in Oakland in 1856. He was a Justice of the Peace in Brooklyn (now a part of Oakland) in 1856 and 1857. He moved to Siskiyou County in 1858, where he purchased a ranch near Fort Jones. He engaged in agricultural pursuits, mining, and the practice of law. He was a member and Sergeant-at-Arms of the California State Assembly in 1865 and 1866. He again served as a member of the Assembly in 1871 and 1872. He married Samantha Jane Patterson (1837-1930) who bore three children, one of whom, Henry, died when he was 8½ years old.

Luttrell was elected as a Democrat from the 3rd District to the 43rd, 44th, and 45th Congresses (1873-1879), but declined to be a candidate for reelection. He resumed the practice of law, farming, and mining, and served as a member of the board of state prison directors from 1887 to 1889. He was appointed United States Commissioner of Fisheries and special agent of the United States Treasury for Alaska in 1893. He died in Sitka, Alaska at age 62, and was interred in Fort Jones Cemetery, Fort Jones, California.

While not related to charcoal-making, it is interesting to note that an 1195-page report of the California Senate Joint Select Committee on Chinese immigration (1862) listed a J.K. Luttrell in Appendix F as an honorary vice-president of the Anti-Chinese Union of San Francisco. According to the organization's constitution, its objectives were "to protect the people of the United States from the degrading influences of Chinese labor in any form; to discourage and stop any further Chinese immigration; to compel the Chinese living in the United States to withdraw from the country; and to unite, centralize, and direct the Anti-Chinese strength of our country to the end that good order and harmony may prevail." It also is recorded that Luttrell while in Congress made a speech to the House of Representatives, titled "The Chinese in America," denouncing Chinese immigration. It was one of those unfortunate periods of xenophobia in U.S. history and apparently Luttrell was caught in its web.

Subsequently, the Chinese Exclusion Act was passed by the U.S. Congress and signed into law by President Chester A. Arthur on May 6, 1882. It was one of the most significant restrictions on free immigration in U.S. history, prohibiting all immigration of Chinese laborers. The act followed revisions made in 1880 (a year after Luttrell's term of office expired) to the U.S.-China Burlingame Treaty of 1868, revisions that allowed the U.S. to suspend Chinese immigration. The act was initially intended to last for 10 years, but was renewed in 1892 and made permanent in 1902. It was not repealed until December 17, 1943 (by the Magnuson Act).

Returning to the history of charcoal production, J. Charles Whatford, an archaeologist from the California Office of Historic Preservation identified a number of circular flats, cut and filled from the naturally sloping terrain - three sites at Trione-Annadel State Park and five sites at Sugarloaf Ridge State Park. The sites at Sugarloaf, discovered between 1969 and 1995, included 12 surface charcoal ovens and the remnants of three access / haul roads, all but two of these were located near or adjacent to seasonal streams and, at several locations, on terraces adjacent to the perennial Sonoma Creek.

The Sugarloaf sites are recorded as:

CA-SON-2143H: Six flats 30 to 40 feet in diameter on a terrace near Sonoma Creek with deposits of black soil and charcoal. The vegetation consists of grassland, overtaken by yellow star thistle, with adjacent hillsides of oak woodland.

Note: The only charcoal production site that is visible to hikers is most likely one of the sites mentioned above. It is located on Grey Pine Trail at the final bend that leads to Sonoma Creek, about 50 yards from the creek. It now is overgrown with chaparral and cut by the trail, but if one scratches around in the dirt, very small remnants of charcoal still can be found.

CA-SON-2144H and CA-SON 2145H: Each site contains a small circular flat about 35 feet in diameter. Both sites are on terraces adjacent to drainages. Site 2144 is grassland, blending into oak woodland. Site 2145 is in an area of mixed evergreen forest with oak, bay, Douglas-fir and madrone.

CA-SON-2147H: This site contains three circular flats connected by remnants of a narrow dirt road along the banks of an intermittent drainage. Cutting and filling of the naturally sloping terrain created all three flats. One flat is located at the toe of a grassy slope near a riparian corridor growing along the watercourse. The second is on a terrace in the "Y" formed where two small drainages meet in an area of mixed evergreen forest. The third flat is situated on a bench cut into the hillside above the confluence.

CA-SON-2148H: This site includes a narrow access / haul road extending about 250 feet along the bank of a drainage to a small circular flat about 25 feet in diameter, located on an alluvial terrace adjacent to an unnamed seasonal creek containing oak savannah.

THE GENTLEMAN RANCHERS

Homesteading in the Mayacamas Ridge (as described in the previous chapter on "Homesteads & Homesteaders") was part of the American and immigrant settlement of the area that occurred in the mid-19th century. The few records that are available are confusing, because many parcels were not registered upon settlement, and many parcels were leased to the actual residents. The small ranch / farm family operations were continually sold or consolidated, and at times lost through bankruptcy.

Some of this land was purchased by individuals who utilized and improved it for ranching operations. Two of these settlements, the Reynolds Ranch and the McCormick Ranch, are prominent in the cultural history of Sugarloaf Ridge State Park.

THE REYNOLDS RANCH

The first family to be associated with the property, that still today is called the Reynolds Ranch, was the Luttrell family, who settled here around 1870. As we saw in the previous chapter, the Luttrell family consolidated several of the surrounding homesteads for the purpose of charcoal production. As well, the family had a small farm operation for raising stock and growing walnuts and subsistence crops. The Luttrells lost ownership of their holdings in the 1890s through mortgage complications. Henry Schwartz claimed the Luttrell lands in 1893 at a sheriff's auction, and then sold it in 1910 to John W. Warboys, who immediately sold the property to W.D. Reynolds.

Reynolds kept the property for only six years; but during that time, he built the main ranch complex and the road that presently is used through Adobe Canyon. (Before building that road, the ranch property was accessed via an older route through Nun's Canyon.) Reynolds also constructed the water system that continues to be used today, as well as bunk houses, sheds and the still-standing white barn. A two-bedroom home (pictured at right) stood across from the present white barn. It was considered unsafe and was razed soon after the park opened.

Some charcoal was produced on the property for a short time, and the land was devoted predominantly to the traditional uses of grazing and farming. It is not known who actually lived in the ranch house. It may have been Reynolds or an overseer, as Reynolds was listed in the 1899-1900 Sonoma County Directory with an office in Santa Rosa at 220 Hinton Avenue, near the old court house, with businesses in real estate, insurance, and notary public documentation. As well, he had at that time another ranch of 1,500 acres near Geyserville.

Reynolds consolidated properties in the area and built his holdings from the original 640 acres to 1,040 acres, which he sold in 1916 to the previous owners, John and Hetty Warboys. Warboys also could be said to have borne the appellation of "gentleman rancher" as he had been in the Santa Rosa area since 1881, and eventually became a leading druggist in town with a store on 4th Street and a residence on the corner of 4th and E streets.

The Reynolds Ranch, as we shall see in the next chapter, was purchased by the State, and later leased for five-year periods for pasture land and dairy operations.

THE MCCORMICK RANCH

William J. Hudson emigrated from Missouri in 1844 and settled in the Los Guilicos area of Kenwood, where he bought 2,500 acres to raise wheat and livestock. His brother Martin joined him and bought an adjacent large ranch. William later purchased a large tract of land in the Napa Valley, which included what is now known as the McCormick Ranch, named for William McCormick, the original ancestor who had settled in the area.

William's son, Henry Mixer McCormick, was given the McCormick Ranch as a wedding present on the occasion of his marriage in 1866 to Mary Jane (Molly) Hudson. There is an interesting "sidebar" concerning Molly and California history: In the spring of 1846, all residents who were not of Spanish or Mexican descent were asked to leave the country. While the McCormicks left for Missouri (only later to return), the Hudsons stayed and became part of the so-called Bear Flag Party. They fashioned several flags depicting bears, one of which is said to have been fashioned from Molly's mother Sarah's petticoat. The Bear Flag Party took possession of the Sonoma Barracks, captured the arms therein, and took the resident officer, Mariano Vallejo, prisoner. Molly had been born in Sonoma at the Adobe across from Mission corner in 1846, the year of the Bear Flag Revolt. The family's oral history maintains that she was the first white child born under the Bear Flag, and was called the "Bear Flag Baby," a distinction for which she received $100 from the Society of California Pioneers.

Henry and Molly built a cabin in the homestead area of the 3,000-acre McCormick Ranch, where they raised sheep and cattle. Henry died in 1879, leaving Molly with five young children between the ages of 3 and 11. She mortgaged the ranch to a relative, and then spent the rest of her life reclaiming it free and clear. After the death of a descendent, Edwin Harding Learned, the ranch was leased to local livestock producers until 1993, at which time the family initiated plans for the eventual transfer of the property to the California State Department of Parks and Recreation for inclusion in Sugarloaf Ridge State Park.

WHERE IS LAKE SUGARLOAF?

As we learned in the previous chapter, 1,040 acres of the Reynolds Ranch had been sold in 1916 to John and Hetty Warboys. The land use remained the same until the Warboys property was purchased by the State of California in 1920. While the land was used for grazing livestock, the overriding value of the property to the State was the watershed of Sonoma Creek, whose headwaters begin in Sugarloaf Ridge State Park. It was the State's plan to divert the waters of the creek to the Sonoma State Home at Eldridge near Glen Ellen.

The Sonoma State Home began life in 1883 as the California Home for the Care and Training of Feeble-Minded Children. It was originally located in Vallejo and was moved in 1885 to the town of Santa Clara. It was charged with caring for children between the ages of five and eighteen who were incapable of receiving instructions in the common schools. Soon after its creation, the facilities were found to be inadequate. In 1891, the 1,660-acre William McPherson Hill farm near the town of Glen Ellen was purchased as the site for a new home. The new site had been suggested by a legislative commission led by Captain Oliver Eldridge, after whom the site was named. The Sonoma State Home functioned for a time as an autonomous institution, serving four types of patients: the mentally handicapped, the epileptic, the physically disabled and the "psychopathic delinquent." It was placed under the Department of Institutions in 1921and later, under the Department of Mental Hygiene. The name of the institution was changed to the Sonoma State Home in 1915, changed again in 1953 to the Sonoma State Hospital, and changed for a final time in 1986 to the Sonoma Developmental Center. At the time of this writing the Sonoma Developmental Center was scheduled to close its doors in December 2018.

Water was a critical resource for the growing State Home; and as early as February, 1920, work had begun on a water diversion project. However, a legal dispute arose with the surrounding property owners and downstream users, who depended on the Sonoma Creek for agriculture and recreation. The opponents eventually won the argument and the project was cancelled. Only later did the Sonoma State Home address its water needs with the construction on hospital property of Lake Suttonfield in 1938 (photo left). The primary outflow into Lake Suttonfield is from Sonoma Creek.

It is interesting to speculate that, had the State won the water rights argument, much of Sugarloaf Ridge State Park might today be known as Lake Sugarloaf.

Although their primary purpose of water diversion was not to be realized, the State Home retained ownership of the former Reynolds Ranch for several more years. Supervisors from the institution and their families stayed at the ranch complex to watch over the animals and also to grow their own crops. The property also provided the opportunity for another initiative: the recreation and development of youth through scouting.

CAMP BUTLER

During the 1930s, while most of the U.S. was mired in the Great Depression, the sounds of youthful laughter mingled with the rustle of leaves and the chirping of birds on the most scenic section of Hillside Trail. They were the sounds of Boy Scouts and Campfire Girls at play at Camp Butler.

Beginning in 1931 and until WWII, the camp was the site of weekend and two-week summer activities for "inmates" of the Sonoma State Home in Eldridge and the children of staff members. The camp was named for Dr. Frederick Otis Butler who served for 31 years as the Superintendent of the Home.

The Boy Scouts were responsible for building the camp, which included a 28x18-foot cookhouse (shown here on the left). The Scouts slept outside in tents. The Scouts also helped to build a tractor-dug, shale-lined swimming pond that was fed by a nearby stream. Across from the pond, a rock-bordered area served as the parade ground for scouting ceremonies.

The fireplace and the outside patio of the cookhouse remain, but the pond (now filled with reeds) and a portion of the parade ground with a hole for the flagpole can be seen on Hillside Trail about 100 yards below the cookhouse ruins.

With the start of WWII, the scouting activities at Camp Butler ceased as fuel supplies were rationed and many of the scouts and their leaders were drafted or enlisted in the war effort. Also, the patient profile at the Sonoma State Home began to change to care for more severely disabled persons. Other wards of the State who had been previously housed at the institution were sent to other facilities.

After the end of WWII and the closure of Camp Butler, the State property was leased for cattle grazing and hunting. Lessees included Wesley (Dutch) and Vivian (Toad) Phister (1943-1948), John Elgard (1948-1951), Frank and Virginia Monnich ((1951-1953), and the Raffo Brothers Milk Transport Company of Glen Ellen (1953-1964).

In 1959, the Reynolds Ranch was declared as surplus property. Its immediate public sale was prevented by the review of state lands for the placement of a North Bay Area state college. This allowed time for public and political forces to martial efforts to make the property a state park.

SUGARLOAF BECOMES A PARK

On September 24, 1964, the Reynolds Ranch property - now up to 1,520 acres - was transferred from the State Department of Mental Hygiene to the California State Division of Beaches and Parks and designated "Sugarloaf Ridge State Park." After construction of an entry road and a campground, and the destruction of several of the Reynolds Ranch buildings, the park was opened to the public on Memorial Day weekend 1969 under the direction of its first resident Ranger, Milo Shepard. Mr. Shepard, whose photo appears here, was the great-grandnephew of Jack London and the executor of his literary estate.

Over the next several years, Sugarloaf Ridge State Park was expanded through a series of purchases and transfers:

1970 - Pacific Telephone and Telegraph transferred 49.5 acres around Red Mountain to the park for an access route to the top of Bald Mountain, and constructed on their remaining five acres a telephone microwave station at the summit of Red Mountain.

1971 - The State purchased the Hurd homestead red barn. The entire Bear Creek Ranch and the 80-acre Malm Flat Ranch were added.

1972 - 40 acres west of the campground owned by Barbara K. Von Tillow were added to the park.

1973 - 150 acres owned by Robert W. Ragle along the west boundary of the park were purchased, adding a quarter mile of Adobe Canyon Road to the park including the summit on Sugarloaf Ridge that is visible from Kenwood, and whose shape gave the park its name.

1979 - In this year, a program was initiated by Margery Stern with the Trust for Public Lands to transfer approximately 330 acres of her ranch west of Bear Creek to the park in small parcels, to be completed by 1988. Along with the purchase of the 60-acre Fiorentino property, a complete connection was made between Sugarloaf Ridge State Park and Hood Mountain Regional Park.

The original ranch house at Stern Ranch was destroyed in the October 2017 fire.

1984 - On January 31, electricity finally arrived at Sugarloaf Ridge State Park.

1985 - 40 acres of Bureau of Land Management land in Napa County along the eastern edge of the park and 5.2 acres known as the Harr Ranch next to Hood Mountain Regional Park were added. The Harr family retained tenancy rights until 1988.

1987- The present Visitor Center was constructed near the campground entrance.

1990 - 1,100 acres of the McCormick Ranch were incorporated into the park, bringing the total park footprint to 4,000 acres.

1997- The Robert Ferguson Observatory was constructed in the group camp area.

THE RANGER DIARIES

Park Rangers - called Park Peace Officers after 1974 - are sworn peace officers who perform a wide variety of duties including law enforcement, emergency medical response, patrol, resource protection, and interpretation of historic, natural and cultural resources. The male and female Rangers assigned or assisting at Sugarloaf Ridge State Park from 1969 to 2012, along with their Park Aides, had maintained hand-written diaries in which they noted the events of each day that they were on duty. Thirty eight of these diaries, covering the period from 1971 to 2012, were found in storage in the Sonoma Barracks and were researched by this author.

The diaries were kept in off-the-shelf 6x9x1-inch or 8x10x1-inch journals labeled as "Daily Diary," "Standard Diary," or "Daily Journal" (see photo sample below).

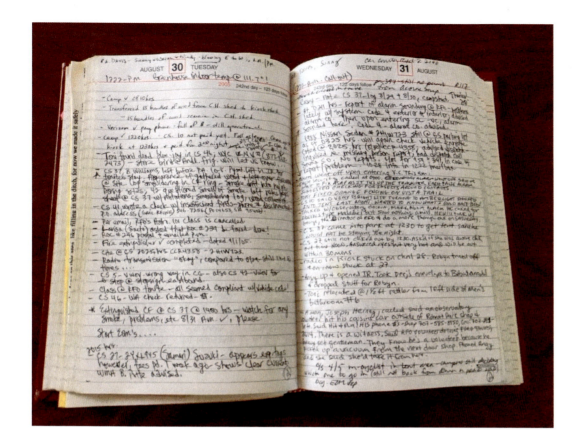

The 38 diaries (3 years were missing) contained more than 13,000 entries, most of which were of middling significance. The first entry on January 1, 1971, was written by Sugarloaf Ridge State Park's first Ranger, Milo Shepard, and stated simply: "Shepard checked out the Park. Everything OK."

Thereafter, the entries were somewhat longer, but no less routine. The diaries recorded activities such as the collection of user fees, maintenance of facilities and vehicles, trail clearing, camper relations, and citations for pet and vehicular violations. Every so often, however, diary entries were found that were out of the ordinary and provided an enhanced perspective on the challenges and joys of park supervision, as well as glimpses into significant milestones that occurred during the first 41 years of park history.

Here, below, is a brief selection from among the 13,000 entries in the Ranger diaries, some of which reflect Sugarloaf's participation in historic events that occurred outside of the park:

November 1, 1975: 50 campsites taken. The large number of out-of-state visitors, particularly from Colorado, appears to belong to some special type of religious group. They are of the unidentified flying object or space ship cult called H.I.M.

H.I.M. was an acronym for Human Individual Metamorphosis. It was the original name of a religious UFO-millenarian group that eventually called itself Heaven's Gate. The group is best known for the 39 members who committed mass suicide in San Diego in 1997, in order to reach what they believed to be an alien space craft following Comet Hale-Bopp. The original followers, about 20 in number, had earlier been sent out in pairs to spread the message. There is evidence that one of the group's recruitment travels took them to "a forest near Santa Rosa."

December 7, 1980: A beautiful day but extremely light day use. Two day-use cars did say they came up from Marin to hike because they were afraid of the killer being on the loose at Mt. Tam.

In 1979-80, "Trailside Killer" David Carpenter murdered one woman and possibly three others on Mount Tamalpais, as well as three women and a man in the Point Reyes National Seashore.

January 3, 1980: A woman in camp site #15 requested that I help capture two blue birds that had been showing up at her site every day. She wanted to mark them for future identification. She said she was sure that they were the same two birds she had seen in other parks. She claimed that they had been following her around the state. Possible? I don't think so.

July 9, 1981: Today the park received two separate accounts of a flying saucer hovering over the campground. It flew from east to west darting above the campground at incredible speed. It then descended below Hood Mountain and lit up the whole horizon. This occurred at approximately 2:07 a.m.; then at 2:30 a.m. it appeared again. It illuminated the clouds and darted and hovered around the campground. It had green, red and amber lights that would blink on and off. Sometimes while hovering it would dart down, zigzag from side to side, and then shoot up and away. The second appearance lasted for 30 minutes; then it darted away never to be seen again.

November 20, 1981: Goodspeed Trail dedication today. A total of 66 persons attended the ceremony including CA State Secretary of Resources Huey Johnson along with representatives from the Trust for Public Lands, Sonoma County Trails Council, Sonoma County Regional Parks, and Youth Conservation Corps. A good time by all.

March 19, 1983: Sugarloaf has had 72.5 inches of rain since July 1982.

The 1982-1983 El Nino was the strongest and most devastating of the 20th century. Rainfall in Santa Rosa that year was nearly 56 inches.

September 2, 1983: Flag is to be flown at half-mast 'til Monday because of international incident involving Russia and its shooting down of a commercial jet liner.

On September 1, a Russian Su-15 interceptor shot down Korean Airlines flight 007 in the Sea of Japan on a flight from New York to Seoul via Anchorage. All 269 passengers and crew were killed.

February 5, 1985: We discovered a pot site and equipment. We removed cans, buckets, fiber pots, chicken wire and shovels. [Ranger] Bill Krumbein took photos.

This is the first diary notation concerning pot growing in the park, which still continues today.

May 17, 1985: Talked to [Supervising Ranger] Larry Ferri about Webb's rabbits. They can keep four as pets. Have removed down to 17. Larry said that would do until the 24th, then four only after Memorial weekend.

The Webbs were regular campers and were a constant challenge for the Rangers. Their camp is pictured at the right. The Webbs were long-stay campers, illustrative of persons referred to in the Ranger diaries as "live-ins." Many of the live-in campers were homeless or on public assistance. This was a problem back in the 1980s that eventually led the Department of Parks and Recreation to institute a two-week maximum stay for campers.

January 28, 1986: Flags went to half-mast - the explosion of space shuttle challenger. 7 dead.

The space shuttle Challenger broke apart 73 seconds into its tenth mission resulting in the deaths of all seven crew members. It was the first of two shuttles to be destroyed in flight, the other being Columbia in 1983. The accident led to a 2.5 year grounding of the shuttle fleet.

Entries for February-May, 1986: 8.92" of rain today. Storm total 22.66." Park closed. Adobe Canyon Road is a real mess. Bridge across creek to Harr Ranch is all twisted out of shape. Parking spaces gone, trees down, retaining wall broken off. Road surface just hanging in mid-air… Sacramento ordered the park closed and all public out until washed out road is replaced.

During 1986, Sugarloaf Ridge State Park was effectively closed for 11 weeks. Pictured on the next page is an Isuzu truck that was washed into Sonoma Creek during one of the rain storms.

July 21, 1986: Retrieved a 2-foot rattler with 10 buttons at campsite #31. Made a great interpretive object for everyone to see in the campground. Took him home and stir-fried him. Actually thought about bringing the wok here; it'd make a nice wok on the wild side.

You gotta love Ranger humor.

May 2, 1992: About 50 bikes and close to 100 people from the Hells Angels. Some of their group stayed at the El Rancho Tropicana motel Saturday night. There was a party night and day - constant traffic into to the group camp and out. They had a drugged-up guard at the group camp checking visitors in. No problem from them. Rangers were on two-at-a time 'till about 2:00 a.m.

Photo right: A Hells Angels biker near the entrance kiosk, heading toward the group camp.

October 24, 1993: Re: Polly search, I hiked from the creek bed area from Gabion's Curve downstream. Nada except trash.

Polly Klaas was kidnapped from her mother's home in Petaluma during a sleepover, and strangled by Richard Allen Davis on October 1, 1993. During the next two months, 4,000 persons were involved in the search for Polly. The Sonoma County Sheriff's Department was assisted by over 500 search team members from 24 agencies, including park Rangers. The search remains today as one of the largest ever conducted in California. On December 4, Davis confessed to kidnapping and murdering Klaas, and led investigators to her shallow grave just off Highway 101a mile south of the city limits of Cloverdale, and about 30 miles from the search site.

February 8, 1997: 5 p.m. dedication of the first wing of the Robert Ferguson Observatory, housing a 40-inch telescope. This is the largest telescope west of the Mississippi that is open to public use. For a probable Sugarloaf record also: in [Ranger] Rich Irwin's 19½ years here, this is the largest single event crowd remembered. Cars were parked into the group camp, at the concession area, along road shoulders from there to the kiosk, at the pay lot, at the visitor center, part way up Stern Trail, and down to upper Canyon / Pony Gate parking.

July 25, 2000: This note was inserted into the diary with the entry for that day: "We camped here during the night of the 22nd until today. While here, a Ranger confiscated my son's samurai sword. We have seen no Ranger this morning. Please save and we will return to pick it up on Aug. 4th."

Now there's an item no camper would want to be without.

HUNTERS, HIPPPIES, HIKERS & HAUNTS

Throughout its long and storied cultural history, the land that is now Sugarloaf Ridge State Park has been inhabited or utilized by a wide variety of persons and groups, beginning with the permanent seasonal settlement of Native American Wappo's 7,000 or more years ago. Following the decimation and displacement of those native peoples, the Mayacamas Ridge attracted an alliterative array of homesteaders, hunters, hippies and hikers.

The story of homesteading in the area of the park has been told above. We know that for a brief period of time one of those homesteads, the Hurd family's Bear Creek Ranch, was purchased by businessmen who used the property as a deer hunting club. Little is known about the actual persons who hunted here; and, so, there are no hunter stories to tell in this narrative.

We learned, as well, in a previous chapter that a number of hippies were said to have been living on the Bear Creek Ranch property; and that in 1968, the old Hurd house was burned to the ground, apparently the result of an untended candle.

Why were hippies here?

HIPPIES IN THE PARK

Hippie interest in Sonoma County can be traced to the Summer of Love in 1967, when the Flower Children who had flocked to San Francisco's Haight-Ashbury District during the previous year began their exodus from the City in a great back-to-the-land movement. The actual date of the decline of the "Hashbury" (as the Haight-Ashbury was called by former Glen Ellen journalist Hunter S. Thompson) is hard to pin down. 1967 seems to be as good a starting date as any. The deaths that year of Woody Guthrie, Alice B. Toklas and Otis Redding, the killing in Bolivia of Che Guevara, the initiation of the "Stop the Draft" movement, and the first U.S. air strike on Hanoi, had cast a wintery chill on the Summer of Love.

According to Patrick McMurtry, a long-time resident of Sonoma Valley, the Summer of Love was the golden window of the hippie movement that "got crusty," leading to an exodus of "psychedelic refugees" from the Haight-Ashbury to Sonoma County. McMurtry told of a "gypsy" group of ten or more persons from the Netherlands, France, Germany and Spain, who were driving around the world in a renovated school bus around 1974-1975. The women were "stunningly beautiful," he recalled. They were among a fluid group living on Cavedale Road in a community of dropouts that was initiated by a man named Rainbow, an engineer who had "chucked it all" to make buttons. The European group eventually left to stay in the Sugarloaf campground because of the lack of a septic system in the Cavedale area.

Jack London State Historical Park docent, Jeff Falconer, recalled a hippie group that in 1967 converted an old vacuum cleaner store in Boyes Hot Springs to a "psychedelic shop." The group, even though in their thirties (remember the axiom, "Never trust anyone over 30"?) influenced the youth of the Sonoma Valley area by their open, attractive, sharing, and let-it-all-hang-out lifestyle. "They had no ideology, were intermittently monogamous and shared admirably," he said. This group was known to have access to various houses and moved nomad-style from one to the other. The Boyes group was considered to be "pretty honest" and might even have rented the Hurd house in Sugarloaf Ridge State Park.

Another hippie hangout was a rented house near the Chateau St. Jean winery. It was used by the band H.P. Lovecraft, a gothic-folk rock group from Chicago that was the biggest name in the valley at that time. Members of the band would occasionally hike into Sugarloaf, according to Jeff Falconer who had camped in the park for an entire month, and who had occasional social contact with them. Falconer's unusually long camping experience at that time was sanctioned by the park's first Ranger, Milo Shepard, perhaps because a section of the original graveled road to the park from Adobe Canyon had washed out after the park opened in 1969, and the only visitors were those who entered the park on foot.

Hippie habitation in Sugarloaf Ridge State Park mirrored the transient structure and flavor of 1960s intentional communities. Hippie activity in the park was loosely organized, with individuals or small groups drifting from place to place to "hang out" in houses located in various places including San Francisco, Santa Cruz, Crooks Creek in Oregon, and Ojo Sarco in New Mexico. Hippie habitation in Sugarloaf never received the kind of notoriety or star quality of Lou Gottlieb's Morningstar Ranch in western Sonoma County, or the Grateful Dead's settlement at Olompali State Park in Marin County.

Hippie habitation is known to have taken place at the Hurd Ranch after it had been sold and subsequently rented or leased, but the number of inhabitants is not known. It was estimated by Ranger Milo Shepard that 30 persons regularly used the road to the house, and that number swelled to as many as 90 on the weekends.

Park volunteer Bill Myers related a conversation with Kenwood resident John Frediani, who indicated that the old Hurd ranch was leased to his father, Larry Frediani, for use as a deer club until it was sold to the State in 1971. "We seldom used the old house because everyone wanted to camp outside," said Frediani. "Hippies, yes they were around. Dad had them living all over the site. They had about four camps set up," he said.

A group was thought to be living at the Hurd house at the time that the house burned in 1968. Former State Senior Archeologist, Breck Parkman, investigated the area around the Hurd house ruins and found that there was a large residency during that time. His most recent findings during

2014 revealed several article, including a woman's sandal, a leather belt with a brass buckle, a colorful knit scarf, and an article of underclothing with embroidered butterflies, reminiscent of the hippie fashions of the 1960s. (See photos on pg. 23.)

The photo above, taken by the author in 2017, pictures a group of Hurd family descendants near the remains of the Hurd family home at Bear Creek Ranch. Only the staircase, a crumbling brick fireplace and the foundation of an outbuilding remain from the 1968 fire that destroyed the residence.

THE HARMONIC CONVERGENCE

In addition to hippie habitation, Sugarloaf Ridge State Park in 1987 experienced a shared Hippie-New Age phenomenon called the "Harmonic Convergence". The Harmonic Convergence is the name that was given to the world's first globally-synchronized meditation, which occurred on August 16-17, 1987; and which also closely coincided with an exceptional alignment of the planets Mercury, Venus and little Pluto (which had not yet been demoted to a dwarf planet). The convergence is purported to have corresponded with a great shift in the earth's energy from warlike to peaceful. Believers of this esoteric prophecy maintained that the Harmonic Convergence ushered in a five-year period of the Earth's "cleansing", during which time many of the planet's "false structures of separation" would collapse.

An important aspect of the Harmonic Convergence observance was the idea of congregating at "power centers" such as Mount Shasta and Mount Fuji, where the spiritual energy was thought to be particularly strong. The global event was popularized by Jose Arguelles, an art historian who wrote "The Mayan Factor: The Path Beyond Technology." Arguelles believed that a minimum of 144,000 people would need to assemble at these and other power centers on Sunday, August 17 "to create a field of trust" and meditate for peace "to ground the vibrational frequencies" that would facilitate the arrival of a new era.

According to news reports, there were as many as 6,000 participants on Mt. Shasta on Sunday, the main day of the Harmonic Convergence. The roads up the mountain were clogged with RVs and buses; traditional camping areas were crowded with tent campers, and every trail had its share of day-pack hikers. It was somewhat of a populist phenomenon, for those present could not be so easily pegged as simply belonging to America's counter culture. Young and old were observed as well as rich and poor, hippie and yuppie (young urban professionals), although most participants seemed to be New Age adherents. Recorders of the Shasta event met astrologers, channelers, and even some "Bible-thumping locals" who drove up to convert the invading New Agers.

Sugarloaf Ridge State Park achieved the stature of a locally-designated power center, as did Mt. Tamalpais in Marin County, Santa Catalina Island, and the Mt. Griffith Observatory in Los Angeles. The following entry in the Ranger diary for August 14, 1987 provides an insight into preparations for the big event at the park: "This is the beginning of the Harmonic Convergence function. A lot of campers came up early and there were a tremendous amount of phone calls. Eight chemical toilets were dropped off for the function. Hum-baby, it's gonna be fun"!

On Saturday, August 16, an evening "purification ceremony" was held to kick off the Sugarloaf observance. Co-organizer, Gabriel Cousens, a psychiatrist, holistic physician, homeopath, Ayurvedic practitioner, Chinese herbalist, and diabetes researcher from Petaluma, said that participants would burn off their negativity by symbolically imprinting it on leaves and throwing them into a campfire. "My anticipation," said Dr. Cousens, "is not that it's going to be a big cosmic boom as much as it's going to be an opening of the door for more positive energy coming into the planet."

Throughout the afternoon of August 16, new arrivals to the park set up camp and prepared for activities to include, on the following day, a Native American medicine wheel, singing, chanting and dancing. Meanwhile the now-reinforced Sugarloaf Rangers worked assiduously behind the scenes to assure a calm, peaceful and well-ordered event. Approximately 1,200 visitors were in the park that day.

Diane Besida, who from 1982 to 2008 served as an assistant caretaker of the Stern Ranch, participated in the Sunday Harmonic Convergence ceremony at Sugarloaf. She recalled that the Sunday observance began in the camping area: "It was incredibly hot that day. We hiked to an open meadow where the ground had been prepared like a medicine wheel. [See photo of a typical medicine wheel at left.] We walked the wheel independently, entering from the east, crossing to the west, then south, then north, then to the center. Whenever someone felt like hiking up to the clearing where the wheel was laid out, they did." At the end of the day following a separate group ceremony, participants were able to select and keep a crystal.

By most accounts, the Harmonic Convergence observances at Sugarloaf were concluded successfully. The Ranger diary for August 17 noted that the last of the participants were "filtering out," and that officials of the event had given Ranger Joe White a small polished marble slab with "Peace" written on it in Japanese characters.

HIKERS

From the day that Sugarloaf Ridge State Park opened in 1969, it has become a magnet for day-users and campers, who engage in independent or organized hikes and who, like John Muir, would no doubt agree that "In every walk with nature one receives far more than one seeks." With its 25 miles of trails, challenging elevations and spectacular views, Sugarloaf is a hiker's paradise.

HAUNTS

Our review of the history of Sugarloaf Ridge State Park turns to the fourth "H" in the title of this chapter: Haunts. As we have seen throughout this narrative, the cultural history of the park is rich, indeed. But there is another side of the park's history, a darker side that involves the deaths of individuals by accident, suicide or foul play.

Incident #1: The Big Boom at Fitzsimmons Ranch

There are very few facts recorded about the first death by suicide in the area that is now Sugarloaf Ridge State Park. All that is known is that a man named Johnson (either a homesteader or a ranch hand) in 1915 committed suicide by the unusual method of blowing himself up. In an interview with Francis and Hazel Hurd, who lived with their parents Ray and Bertha and their siblings on the Hurd Ranch homestead, Francis said that, "We had some neighbors by the name of Johnson and there was, I know, two kids in that family, and I think they lived on the Fitzsimmons Ranch. But anyhow, Mr. Johnson decided he had enough of this life, and he took a stick of dynamite and went out on one of them rock outcroppings or stumps and lit the fuse and sat down on it."

Incident #2: A Plane Crash Near Brushy Peaks

On December 10, 1964, Long Beach oilman, Clinton A. Petrie, age 48, landed his blue and silver twin-engine Cessna 310 aircraft at the Nut Tree Airport in Vacaville for refueling. Petrie had departed Long Beach a few hours earlier and was headed for Santa Rosa, where he was scheduled to pick up two potential investors for his struggling oil company and fly them back to Long Beach. It was almost time to make payroll and Petrie and the oil company he owned were having a hard time making ends meet. With the money from some new investors in the company's account, the payroll could be made. Clinton Petrie was on a mission to keep everything together. (Petrie's Cessna 310 would have looked like the model pictured above.)

When he departed Vacaville around 10:30 in the morning, Petrie radioed the airport in Santa Rosa. The controller who answered advised Petrie that the weather was deteriorating and that a winter storm was rolling in. Petrie was an experienced pilot, but he was not instrument certified. In spite of the bad weather, Petrie continued on toward Santa Rosa, following a route that would take him over the Mayacamas Mountains. At about 11:00 that morning, in zero visibility, Petrie slammed his aircraft into the top of a ridge near Brushy Peaks in the park. Although dozens of planes from the Civil Air Patrol were sent out to search for the crash site, it wasn't until after the weather had improved on December 12 that the remains of the plane were found. (The photo on the previous page shows some of the remains of Petrie's plane.)

Incident #3: The Skull in Bear Creek

It was close to dark on October 30, the day before Halloween 1980, when Greg Gilbert and his wife, who were hiking cross-country in the area near Bear Creek, wandered onto a surprising find. "We were about a third of a mile from Adobe Canyon Road and about 500 feet down into the canyon, when we saw what looked like a large puffball. When we went to look at it, we came face-to-face with a grimy human skull," said Greg. There were also a number of non-human bones scattered about the area in no recognizable pattern. Greg took the lower jawbone of the human skull for evidence; but reconsidered, thinking that it ought to remain exactly where it was found.

Once out of the canyon, he reported his find to the Sonoma County Sheriff at a nearby sub-station, and a detective was dispatched to investigate the matter. Greg gave his statement to the detective; and, because he had hiked the area more than his wife, was asked to ride with the detective in the Sheriff Department's helicopter to spot the site from the air. "A detective later called and told us that they had identified the remains by finding a wallet near the site where the bones were found," he said. The wallet contained the I.D. of a Mr. Scott Peterson and approximately $1,000 dollars. The detective could find no probable cause of death by violence, suicide or animal attack; and had placed the approximate time of death at from six months to two years prior to the Gilbert's discovery.

Peterson was identified as having been born in 1953 in Longmont, Colorado, which is located in northeastern Boulder County, 34 miles from downtown Denver. The detective had located and talked with Peterson's parents, who still lived in Longmont; and they had requested contacting the Gilberts. "They subsequently called and we spoke with them at some length, 30-60 minutes, I guess. They wanted to know all about the area in which the remains were found, and more about Sonoma County," said Greg. "Interestingly, it turned out that the parents and my wife knew some people in common from the Longmont area," he added.

Gilbert discovered from the elder Peterson's that Scott had been a member of the Unification Church. He was a "Moonie." He had told his parents that his spiritual advisors requested that he not speak with them, and had not done so for a year. Gilbert had heard stories of a Moonie encampment along Trinity Road or Cavedale Road, south of Sugarloaf Ridge State Park during the period 1970-1974; and had observed a group of Moonies selling flowers at the corner of Napa Road and 8th Street East in Sonoma.

He also recounted the story of a former friend that he and his wife encountered by chance at a nightclub in Cotati. "She was skittish, like on a psychedelic trip. She feared for her life and was looking for a safe haven," he said. The Gilbert's friend had been a member of the Unification Church in Texas and had risen to become a bookkeeper. In that privileged position, she had become aware of an income of $50,000 a week, ostensibly from selling flowers - an amount large enough to raise her curiosity, if not suspicion. She questioned the income and became, she said, the victim of "sexual shenanigans" against her. She shared her concerns with a close associate, who later "disappeared," which for Gregg validated stories about rumored Moonie killings.

Incident #4: A Suicide in the Campground

On December 27, 1985, Ranger Rich Irwin was called at home at 10:00 in the evening by the Sheriff's Department to respond to a reported suicide in the park. In the late afternoon, 52-year old Mr. Elmer L. Jenner drove into the park, parked his car backed-in at camp site #23, and hooked up a newly-purchased hose to his car's exhaust.

In a note that he had left, Mr. Jenner indicated that he had been thinking about committing suicide for at least two days. (According to a park volunteer who had worked at Sonoma Developmental Center, Mr. Jenner had been a psychiatric technician at that institution. He had been accused of sexually molesting a client, and had gone to Sugarloaf before the start of his scheduled court trial.)

A neighboring camper had called the Sheriff after noticing the car idling for so long, with window glass fogging up. Deputies arrived after 9:30 P.M., and then called for the coroner, the Ranger, a tow truck, and the mortuary. The Sheriff's office and the coroner had collected the physical evidence and had taken photos by the time Ranger Irwin arrived. Other campers were asleep at the time.

Incidents #5 & #6: The Bodies in Sonoma Creek

During the late 1980s or early 1990s, the intact body of a murdered female, possibly a prostitute and possibly a "mob hit," was found by Ranger Paul Larsen below Vista Point as a result of his observation of what looked to be, from above, a mannequin. No evidence of the foul deed was found.

Another corpse, described by retired Ranger Robyn Ishimatsu as a "body dump," was discovered in the creek below Vista Point before the start of her stewardship in 1995. She checked with retired Trione-Annadel State Park Ranger, Bill Krumbein, who added, "The Sheriff's Office came up and retrieved that body and did the investigation. I never viewed the body. It was dark when I got there. The bad guys - a woman and a man - shot this guy while he was asleep in bed, then hauled the body, bed linens and all, to Sugarloaf and pitched him over the side at the overlook parking spot on the entrance road."

Incident #7: Death in an Emerald Glade

It was, literally, a dark and stormy night in December 2002, when Senior State Archeologist Breck Parkman heard a knock on the door of his mobile home in Sugarloaf Ridge State Park. "It was pouring down rain and I thought, who knocks on the door at 11:30 p.m.? But I had to open it," he said. Standing on the front deck were two State Park Rangers, Bob Birkland and Noel Wardell, who had been dispatched to follow up on a call that had been made to the State Highway Patrol concerning a reported suicide in the park.

Breck had noticed two Highway Patrol cars leaving the park when he returned home earlier that evening, but had not given it much thought. The patrols had been following up on a note that was left in the home of a man who proclaimed that he was going to the "Ceremony Tree" in Sugarloaf Ridge State Park with the intention of performing an ancient Celtic suicide ritual, which involved stripping naked and then dying from exposure. The man's car was found at the Goodspeed Trail parking lot, but no trace of the man himself was found by the patrolmen; so, State Parks was called to assist with their knowledge of the park trails and boundaries.

The two Rangers at Parkman's front door in the drenching rain were there to inquire about the whereabouts of that Ceremony Tree. Breck had not heard of such a tree; and, so, Birkland took off in the park's ATV, and Wardell went on foot to search the trails. By 3:00 a.m., with the man's car still at the Goodspeed Trail lot, no trace of him was found. After daybreak, a team of six Rangers arrived to assist in the search. The body of a man about 55 to 60 years old eventually was found hanging from a tree limb behind the Big Leaf Maple tree (i.e., the so-called Ceremony Tree) located on the Headwaters Trail, a few hundred yards from its junction with Vista Trail. Apparently, the comparatively mild weather conditions in the park were not conducive to a death by exposure.

Several years later in 2013, Breck and his son were exploring the area where the suicide occurred. While climbing a tree, the son discovered in the crook of some limbs a rusty pin displaying a Bible passage from Romans 1:16, which read, "I am not ashamed of the gospel as it is the power of God" (photo left) When had it been left and by whom? Was it left by the victim? Was it part of a Christian rite by family or friends intended to spiritually "cleanse" the area? Or was it just an unrelated discovery?

Hikers along the Headwaters Trail near Vista Trail will pass by the spot where the 2002 suicide occurred, perhaps unaware of the drama that unfolded there not so many years ago. The area, thanks to Sugarloaf Ridge State Park volunteer Dave Chalk, now is marked on the park map with an asterisk.

Incident #8: A Heart Attack on a Group Hike

The popular Bill and Dave Hikes have long attracted large numbers of ardent hikers. It was on one of their hikes in Sugarloaf Ridge State Park in 2001, about a week after the 9/11 terrorist attack on the Twin Towers, that hike leader Dave Chalk received an urgent walkie-talkie alert from Bill Myers, who was acting that day as sweep. The hike had just begun and had reached the amphitheater near the Creekside Nature Trail when Bill radioed, "Get back here, Dave, we have a problem."

One of the hikers, a man about 49 years of age from Windsor, was down and was turning blue. There were several medically trained people on the hike including a nurse and a paramedic, who provided emergency care, while another person called 911. Within 15 minutes an ambulance arrived, but the man was by then "as blue as a pair of blue jeans," said Dave. Resuscitative efforts failed and the body eventually was transported away. Some hike participants left at that point, but others stayed to finish the hike.

"I was feeling bad wondering, what if anything could have been done differently," said Dave Chalk. "A couple of days later, the Ranger told me that he thought nothing could have been done to save the man." Sometime later, on a United Express flight from Santa Rosa to the San Francisco airport, Dave chanced upon a fellow passenger, a physician, who turned out to be the victim's doctor. Apparently, the man had been treated for diabetes and, according to the doctor, "It was his time to go and nothing more could have been done."

Incident #9: A Suicide off Hillside Trail

Former Ranger Robyn Ishimatsu recalled responding to a probable suicide off Hillside Trail around the period of 2002-2004. A couple of hikers had gone off the trail, and had found and subsequently reported their discovery of a fairly intact skeleton, fully-clothed in men's attire. The man was discovered to have been missing for several months from another area in California. He had left a suicide note at his home, which indicated that he was "going to Sugarloaf to shoot myself." However, there were no visible gun wounds, nor was a weapon found. The police investigators subsequently wrote off the incident as a suicide.

SUGARLOAF IN ITS GOLDEN YEARS

Memorial Day weekend 2019 will mark the 50th anniversary of public access to Sugarloaf Ridge State Park. In 2012, management of the park was awarded to Team Sugarloaf, a not-for-profit entity, under the terms of a seven-year contract with the California State Department of Parks and Recreation. The team that comprises Team Sugarloaf included the Sonoma County Ecology Center, the Valley of the Moon Natural History Association, the Sonoma County Trails Council, the Valley of the Moon Observatory Association, and United Camps, Conferences and Retreats. Their concerted effort assured that Sugarloaf would not be one of the 55 State parks that were earmarked for closure due to budgetary reasons. The original management contract with Team Sugarloaf was scheduled to end at the end of 2019.

A commission established in 2015 by Governor Jerry Brown - the Parks Forward Commission - recommended in its final report a rededication to working with park partners, like Team Sugarloaf, as well as expanded opportunities for all Californians to access the State's system of 279 parks and 15,000 campsites.

At the time of this writing, the partnership between the State of California and Team Sugarloaf has been successful, and has ushered in a second transformation of the park. The first transformation occurred in 1964, when the property owned by the Sonoma State Home was transferred to the California Division of Beaches and Parks and designated as Sugarloaf Ridge State Park. Under the management of park Rangers, the parkland was prepared and improved to include the construction of a campground and a parking lot; the development of a network of hiking trails; the construction of a visitor center; the razing of several unused buildings, thought to be unsafe; and the day-to-day management of park operations.

The second transformation under the stewardship of Team Sugarloaf, has included the construction of a trail for the physically handicapped; the rebuilding of trails affected by the October 2017 fires; maintenance of roads, culverts, walls, and bridges; an increase in the number of park volunteer hours; the addition of several active fundraising events, field trips, natural history, and cultural history hikes; and a park-to-park shuttle service for hikes between Sugarloaf and the adjacent Hood Mountain Regional Park.

In concert with the recommendations of the Parks Forward Commission concerning access, the Team Sugarloaf partnership has resulted in a sizeable increase in the number of park visitors. Future plans include enhanced outreach to ethnic populations, including the creation of monthly Spanish-language nature and history hikes, and a program of free access for high school clubs and groups.

As Sugarloaf Ridge State Park evolves into its golden years, the need for responsible stewardship continues to be of utmost importance and social value. Protection of parkland and access to its wonders is a societal imperative, for as John Muir has written:

> *"Everybody needs beauty as well as bread, places to play in and pray in, where nature may heal and give strength to body and soul."*

REFERENCES

Note: Detailed references can be found in the papers written previously by the author and cited below.

Driver, Harold, *Wappo Ethnography*. University of California Publications in American Archeology and Ethnography, Volume 36, No. 3, pp. 179-220, University of California Press, Berkeley, California, 1936

Gresham, Linda (Unit Ranger), *Hurd Family Oral History.* August 27, 1983

Inventory of the Department of Mental Hygiene, Sonoma State Hospital Records

Jones, Christina, *Sugarloaf Ridge State Park (An Historic Sketch) Draft*. Cultural Heritage Section, California Department of Parks and Recreation, April 1977

Maniscalco, Lawrence, *Hippies in the Park*. July 2014

Maniscalco, Lawrence, *The Ghosts of Sugarloaf.* November 2014

Maniscalco, Lawrence, *The Charring of Sugarloaf: Charcoal-Making in Sugarloaf Ridge State Park*. March 2015

Maniscalco, Lawrence, *Our First Skywatchers: Native American Astronomy in Sugarloaf Ridge State Park*. April 2015

Maniscalco, Lawrence, *Homesteading in Sugarloaf Ridge State Park*. September 2015

Maniscalco, Lawrence, *Sugarloaf Ridge State Park Unit History 1971 to 2012: Excerpts from the Sugarloaf Ridge State Park Ranger Diaries*. October 2016

McCormick Family Historical Papers

Sand, Dallyce R., *Kenwood Yesterday and Today*. 100th Birthday Edition, Revised 1988

Made in the USA
Las Vegas, NV
28 August 2021